Small Hands

Small Hands

Mona Arshi

First published 2015 by
Liverpool University Press
4 Cambridge Street
Liverpool
L69 7ZU

British Library Cataloguing-in-Publication data
A British Library CIP record is available

ISBN 978-1-78138-181-6 softback

Typeset by Carnegie Book Production, Lancaster
Printed and bound by Booksfactory.co.uk

in memory of my brother,

Deepak Arshi (1971–2012)

Contents

The Lion

How unstable and old he is now.
    Lion, like God, has snacks sent up

by means of a pulley. Although
    you can never master the deep language

of Lion, I am made dumb by the rough
    stroke of his tongue upon mine.

Nowadays I make allowances. We lie
    together and I hear the crackle of his bones

and when I bring myself to open my eyes
    he weeps, his pupils resembling dark

embroidered felt circles. Sometimes
    I think all I am is a comfort blanket for his

arthritic mouth. But many evenings he'll sit
    twisted behind the drapery solving my

vulgar fractions with nothing but his claws.
    Lion and I break bread; I tend to his mane and

he sets a thousand scented fuses under my skin.
    He starts undressing me under the sweetening stars.

Please girl, he mews; this might be the last time
    I will see how the thin light enters you.

Entomological Specimens

Simply leaving specimens in a cyanide jar for a while
sometimes will relax them, but this method is not reliable.

Centre of Insect Systematics

You will need to be pinned in the mid-
dle of your thorax. And, darling, did
you know, that gin is preferable to vodka
in the relaxing jar? I once saw butterflies
mounted by an amateur; glassed too late –
they became infested by tiny insects.
I look over and you are transfixed,
composed. Perhaps it's all the order,
the systems in this quiet and simple
world of corpses? Later, I saw spliced
spiders displayed on framed plastic slides.
I am choosing a pair of lashes that
I will wear for you. In the corner of
my eye I thought I saw one twitch.

Practising Your Skills

I woke and my arm had died in the dark.
I shook it awake,
Waiting for pink plush to resurface.
You always said I had a tendency to catastrophise everything;
I've decided to escape from myself.
On the high shelf behind a jar I let a spider work.
You insist on holding up my elbow as an exhibit,
You're using interrogative pronouns and Latinate speech.
Look into my eyes and tell me about the semi-lunar
Notch of the Ulna.
I want to tell you about the elegant savagery of my spider.
Instead I sit you close whilst I sketch an incoherent moon.

Insomniac

Never marry an insomniac. You will have
              to mind yourself.
                    Have hem weights
        sewn into the lining of your garments,

cure your skin with almond oil until it's bloated
              and the pores are brimming.
                    Purchase a large wooden-grained
        trunk and place it near your bed – it's for

safekeepings. (Obscurely, somewhere deep inside you
              know all this). Very soon
                    you won't be able to tell
        the days apart, you'll develop a tic and it will

distill at the centre (within the hive of your other small
              anomalies). You'll flail
                    in mild wind and when you speak
        minute silver-fish will consort in the pit of your throat.

Exquisite wife to the shade: the exact point you place
              your finger-tip on winter mornings,
                    a raindrop will later stop and fret.
        It's a wonder if you survive at all.

It will all end in the mouth; you'll blink,
              he'll stir. You'll practise lying very very still.
                    Peacock feathers
        (your talismans) will blink back in their jars.

Taster

I taste it because it might taste of honey. I taste it because my brain is a hive. I taste it because I'm properly assimilated. I taste it because I was an only child and refused to share the oranges in the playground. I taste it because I never travelled. I taste it because I've travelled to the frozen tundra of the Northern Arctic. I taste it because of the lack, I taste it because of the surplus. I taste it because Auntie Naveen's best friend tasted it and she never looked back. I taste it because I pity it (to some degree). I taste it because it smells nice. I taste it because of shavings of bones on the wind. I taste it because it might be like the first time (though it's never like the first time).I taste it because I'm perfumed, shameless, godless. I taste it because I'm curious, because of its integrity, its shape, its asking to be tasted. I taste it because I'm scared. I taste it because I don't want to be scared anymore. I taste it because I'm gagging on all the departures. I taste it because of salt. I taste it because nothing is as holy as intimacy because I want it to purr and stink inside me. I taste it because I'm on a civilising mission. I taste it because of Japan. I taste it because I miss the children. I taste it because I tilted the baby last night, gave her a name and forgot it. I taste it because I'm losing my verbs. I taste it because this morning, I saw the first crocus push through the earth and it was yellow. With my tongue I taste it.

What Every Girl Should Know Before Marriage

after Sujata Bhatt

Eliminating thought verbs is the key to a successful marriage.

You're better off avoiding the reach for specificity and
curbing your interest in the interior of things.

The cobra always reverts to TYPE, tuneless
girls tend to wither on the vine.

Oil of jasmine will arouse river fish.

In the poetry of the Sung Dynasty the howling of monkeys
in gorges was used to express profound desolation.

Things you should have a good working knowledge
of: mitochondria, Roman roads, field glasses, making
rice (using the evaporation method only).

When your mother in law calls you smart,
it's not meant as a compliment.

The lighter her eyes, the further she'll travel.

Always have saffron in your kitchen cupboard
(but on no account ever use it).

*Taunt the sky during the day; the stars
will be your hazard at night.*

Do not underestimate the art of small talk. Learn some stock phrases such as 'they say Proust was an insufferable hypochondriac' or 'I'm confident that the Government will discharge their humanitarian obligations.'

Fasting sharpens the mind and is therefore a good time to practise reverse flight.

Your husband may not know you cheated with shop-bought *garam masala* but God will know.

Bad Day in the Office

Darling, I know you've had a bad day in the office
and you need some comfort
but I burned the breakfast again this morning
and the triplets need constant feeding –
they are like little fires. And the rabbit …
the rabbit topped himself but not before
eating the babies and the mother stared at me
as if I was the one who did it!
Everywhere there is the stink of babies and it's a good job
I can't smell my fingers as they've been wrapped
in those marigolds for weeks.
The mother-in-law has been. She didn't stay,
just placed a tulsi plant on the doorstep
with a note saying she had high hopes of it
warding off those poisonous insects.
That estate agent arrived for the purposes of the valuation.
He dandled the babies on his lap and placed his index finger
on my bottom lip. There's some paperwork somewhere.
As for dinner, well that's ruined. Those chillies you sent for
from Manipur? The juice from the curry bored a hole
in the kitchen tiles and I've had to move the pot to the stump
at the bottom of the garden, next to the dock-leaves;
it was a short trip but it was good to get some air.
We need to keep reminding ourselves that when it rains
it is not catastrophic it is just raining.
The lady radio announcer has addressed me on several
        occasions,
– did you know orangutans are running out of habitat
and we don't have much time?

I've become quite adept at handling the eccentric oranges,
those root vegetables need sweating out ... but it's difficult
to concentrate when that sodding bunny blames me
though how could I have done it when all morning
I've been next to the stove stirring the damn pot?
The salsify is eye-balling me, it's lying on top
of that magazine article – *Bored with the same old winter veg?*
Give salsify a go. We promise, you'll never look back.

You Are Not

You are not the ageing tortoise shell. You are not
the pillows of my hands.

You are not the metallic taste in my mouth
when I wake
        (though you could be those threads
        running underneath my tongue).

I doubt you are the strands of hair which survive
on my windowsill
        (and are likely to have lost their
        film of neem oil).

Though you could be the windowpane itself, which
allows me the view of the sky;
        the interesting birds.
        (You are not the birds).

You are not hidden in bone, you do not bloom
in the marrow,
You are (in my opinion) not the rain in November
that studs my scalp.

        (But you might be the heat pressing
      against my body in the market souk
   near the mosaic-mirrored shisha stall).

You are not the sacred cow, a murmur in the heart
or blood-spit in the sink.
If I open my book you might well be the fly's open
wing dashed on the page.

You are not the hand of god on an incoherent
foetal face.

But yes, I think you might be that moment
when the clouds ripen
            (just before the rain,
        before it hits the cloth of my dress,
    my cold hands).

The Gold Bangles

In my bedroom dresser, in a little red box
sit two gold bangles.
They are pure yellow gold
and the pair are a set, though I believe
they once belonged to part of a bigger set
some time ago.
They were given to my grandmother
and passed down to my mother
upon her marriage.
They are very simple, wide bands and
wear and age have pitted the surface
and begun to affect
the integrity of their modest design.
I imagine they were the kind of thing
that could be melted down
and refashioned into more ornate jewellery
or sold by weight quite easily
depending on the circumstances.
I believe many girls at the time
in those Punjabi villages
would have been presented with similar items
by their parents before they departed
on their long journeys.
My mother wore them on her journey to England.
When I hold them in my hands
I like to think not of that long period
when she owned them
but the time before that,
her waiting for *Papaji*
by the gate (like so many other gates)
her wrists,
still unadorned and naked.

My Mother's Hair

My mother's thin salwar
       gives her away.
   Her plait snakes
across her back
        and turns
to whispers at the ends.

Can we touch it?
          they ask in the icy playground.
She shyly places the dark coil
            in their hands.

After bathing,
       it is transformed,
the rope, released
      from its binding fibres,
            falling in

a heavy curtain
          on to her shoulders.
Steaming by the old radiator,
         she sits
         with her pan of dried pulses,
          discarding
         tiny masquerading stones.

'Jesus Saves'

Hounslow High Street, 1979

I am nine and pulling along my brother, dreaming
about Joanne Stubbs who'd holidayed in Broadstairs,
who was ushered to the front of St Luke's Church that morning.

My mother tells me to look the other way as we pass
the pigeon man in the square outside *Brentford Nylons*.

He's now climbed onto a box encrusted with bird droppings;
his face is red and weathered, his hands hold a small brown book.
The eyes are fixed on the distance, beyond the beyond.

And when we pass by a few hours later, he hasn't shifted
from his hardwood spot, he's jousting the air with his fingers,
and though it was long after Enoch, the notes fasten in my head,
that we couldn't be saved, that every last one of us was damned.

Ticking

i.m. Diane Pretty

They lead me (nervous and suited)
to the living room. She's all
peachy-toed and Rimmel red-
mouthed smiles. Machines grind
and wink, but if you listen with care
you can hear that her body
is ticking, then cracking and oozing
out her liquid life, onto the carpeted floor.
She is now an interpreter of silence,
can read the walls' unease,
reveal why the silvery sounds of dawn
rasp just for her. She is aware
that she is being edited, imperceptibly
nibbled by tiny fish, and contracting
down to this verse, this line
in the papers *I am Diane, help me.*

On Ellington Road

Old man Harvey, with his thick specs and polished shoes shouting *trespassers*, yet offering us a penny for collecting his waspy pears.

"*Biji*", looking old in widow-white, whose soft hands were always stained with turmeric.

The achingly cool white brothers, who lived opposite with their Mum and spent days fixing their motor-bikes.

Aunty Kamel, knocking on our door, with her black plait undone, begging us to keep her for the night.

The Aroras, who had a real football pitch at the back of their garden (Hounslow FC).

Cunny, Pummy, Bally, and Kully (all boys).

The girl next door stealing her dad's razor and showing me how to shave my legs with baby oil.

The white-haired lady we called 'Mum' at number 4, roaming the fenceless gardens, until they brought her back in.

Dave, our young lodger, with his paisley cravat, smelling of Brut *and* he had a car.

The boys in the gardens interrupting cricket games to scream at the sky while Concorde flew by. The girls being told off for climbing trees because 'it was dangerous for girls'.

Meeting Renu, the new bride for my mum's cousin, and being scared for her as I'd heard about what had happened in the launderette the year before.

Manjit, aged 9, left in India as a baby arriving back to her parents, her eyes black with *kajal*.

Several men from along the road setting up in our garden and building the extension in just one day.

My dad, insomniac shift-worker, blood-eyed, nursing his head in our tiny kitchen.

Cousin Migrant

She came from the skies, and tells tales of a black sun.
They say she's been with child for fourteen months,
so we're to stop feeding her the tamarind extract,
guava juice and powder from Dr Nirmal's.
She's essentially a home-body.
I've taught her draughts and the metaphysics of presence;
she'll stay as long as she needs.
Her arms are as thin as margins yet she can lift my children
with ease and do *fly-fly* with them in the garden.
She's unpersuaded by science, my anatomy lessons
are just crude drawings
and she thinks our doctors have terrible hands.
She believes in butter for burns, that flat stones never lie
and replaces everything with ginger.
The boys on the market stall love her. Her *dupatta* never slips.
She covers her mouth when she laughs, though her teeth
are perfect white pegs (more perfect than mine).
Someone long ago taught her to listen but not with her ears.
She is the sum of all her parts. Her face is moon:
there are plantings everywhere.
Each night she reassembles herself.
She holds court, cross-legged on the kitchen floor.
She can define emptiness for me in less than ten syllables.
She says everything should be simmered to a thick reduction.
Girls like you are a storm in a tea-cup.

The Daughters

My daughters have lost
two hundred and thirty-six teeth
and counting.
They possess so many skills: they can
craft sophisticated weaponry such as blow-pipes,
lances and slings and know what the sharp end
of a peacock's feather is for.
Last month they constructed a canoe
and saved the *Purdu Mephistopheles* from extinction.
They may not know that a bird in the hand
is worth noting but have learned
never to bleed on any of the auspicious days
and are aware that pleasure
is a point on a continuum.
I fear they will never make good brides,
they are too fond of elliptical constructions
and are prone to lying in the dirt reading
paragraphs in the clouds.
Their shadows are long.
They know many things, my girls;
when they are older I will teach them
that abundance and vulcanisation
are bad words.
When they sleep, they sleep heavy;
I go into their rooms and check their teeth.

Different Principles of Enclosure

Watch the bird with me,
                the start of something,

a whirring crocus,
           little thing
           of spongy moss

climbing
    a paper portrait and
mounting,
          further diminishing

like a pebble
    being sucked down
or drilling,
    exiled in a frame
              of fraying clouds

(stops of breath, sparrow diction,
            hairpin bends in dreams),

all the while acquiring the subtlety
            of winter
            and winter oak

(unwrap the image of the blue felt hat I
          always wore on the heath)

because sometimes flying can be
         like that
         (like the thing that calls you back),
         flushing
            towards memory.

Day Ghost

My day ghost is blooming.
  The invisible guest at my
breakfast table is no interloper,
  she fixes her place every morning.

I've tried offerings of sunlight,
  neatly detached crows' wings,
smooth white china cups.
  But she just sits rapping her

fingers on my surfaces, tears
  strips of paper out of books,
provocative little acts like trying on
  my boots and everywhere leaving

that heavy, sweet scent dripping
  her oily griefs. I cannot give her
what she wants. I'll watch her
  rehearse: swimming up stairwells

but never quite … later in bed, reading
  my book on temples, I apply hand cream,
reflecting on her day, knowing how
  she hates the smell of hawthorn.

This Morning

There's a beginning
            of a thread

like the saffron strands
            on my mother's

hand's on six yards
            of white cotton.

I'm in the garden, almost
            forgotten beside
                the impossible flowers.

The Bird

She's a prize forager.
An assortment of beetle wings are arranged
like shiny badges under her bed.

Her meal worms have been freeze-dried with such care
that they twitch in the bowl
when resurrected with just a speck of water.

She smells of ... preening oil, salt, top notes of earth.
My mother is turning bird.
This tiny, impossible thing

perched in my hand,
molecules exciting her eyes.
Then the soft *click-click* that unlocks

her humanity, she separates from the tips of my fingers,
hops to the gap in the window,
leaving complex glitter in my palm.

Almost September

Through the window she counts five types
of shadow and a pattern in the lower sky;
the child in a tea-stained dress.
She interrupts the solid line of ants with her palm,
herding them towards the ledge.

Outside, the Catholic bee-keeper
who hid his hands all winter
has buried them
in the borrowed light of the hive.
Sometime this afternoon,

the sky will darken and there will be
tiny licks of mania on the pane.
Upstairs, wrapped in bee hum,
I'm staring at my reflection,
plucking my eyebrows in the tattered light.

Phone Call on a Train Journey

The smallest human bone in the ear
        weighs no more than a grain of rice.

She keeps thinking it means something
        but probably is nothing.

Something's lost, she craves it
        hunting in pockets, sleeves,

checks the eyelets in fabric.
        Could you confirm you were his sister?

When they pass her his rimless glasses,
        they're tucked into a padded sleeve;

several signatures later,
        his rucksack is in her hands

(without the perishables),
        lighter than she had imagined.

Small Hands

We've managed to cover the carpets
    with the sheets. We spend a long time
on this task, stretching, pressing the fabric,
    passing our palms over creases.

When we're done the small room
    seems to have swollen with light.
Soon the white sheets will fill with quiet
    bodies. They'll slip off their shoes

before they enter. I'll shift around
    on my knees to cover the exposed floor.
Someone will place his hand on my head:
    an older relative who'll ask for my mother.

Someone will say, 'All March it hasn't rained
    and now the rain comes.' We'll drink
sweet tea. She'll be tapping the glass:
    only her knuckles illuminated.

In the Coroner's Office

Someone
is talking to me
about
my brother's body.

She doesn't know
in a certain light his
hair

took the colour of
blue-black ink
and how he would

wind himself
around my mother's body
to sleep.

She doesn't
know he was
born with
one

ear-lobe curled
tight
as a shell;
how she refused

the doctors and used
those first hours
to press
the new
skin flat.

April

Brave things are happening
        in the garden when I'm not looking.

The junction of each branch
                holds its sobriety.

Frost no longer attempts to fasten
        onto the deepest roots,

but still I'm not sure about trusting
        myself with the distances.

In the house, they come to terms.
        The youngest has gone;

the rooms vibrate, my father weighs
        his son's glasses in his hands.

The word they use for zero is *shunya*.
        They come to terms with its blank centre.

18th of November

In our mother's garden only a few leaves
              are left now and the sun is quivering
          through the branches. Happy Birthday,

brother boy. Are you already eight months gone?
              We measured days like our mother
          measures rice methodically in the dent

of her palm. Last night I dreamt of our childhood
              home, filled with spectral figures
          only the furniture was vivid, and you.

You'll want to know that the garden has been
              kind to us, because the house has not.
          From here, by our old swings, how easy it is

to forget and to see you stepping outside to the patio
              blinking behind your spectacles,
          on the 18th of November, your birthday,
          a newspaper dangling from your hands.

Notes Towards an Elegy

i.
Entirely occupied. A million throats
migrate towards my ribs,
secrete syllables in my chest.
All pores and openings have acquiesced.
I'm slurring in my sleep.

ii.
The accumulation of departures,
mornings of staring down light.

Blame the bend in the trees.
Blame the abstract.
Blame my stupid dumb hands.

iii.
I've forgotten what silence feels like.
Tongue loosened with no protest,
my other tongue, a ceramic figurine,
presses against my teeth.

iv.
What I know is that I'm straining to name the parts,
have failed to name the parts of the poem.

v.
The back of my hand inscribed with dates
are like the hands of a small-boned boy,
sitting under the twitching shade of a tree.

vi.
We found the stumbling bird together
and hand-fed her with white bread soaked in milk.

We had to leave her by the green shed and she did die.
You noted the delicate integrity of its fretwork.

vii.
Wait fast ghost, you should see how the living room is
choked with living things and your mother is upstairs
sitting on your bed, nurturing scraps in the poor light.

The Urn

Closing her eyes she wondered if
she could fit into the tiny gaps though nothing
could be fixed in this remoteness.

In this particular light under which she sits
she considers inbetweenness:
if she moved it slightly to the right

it would be closer to the daffodils.
Her arm hesitates and she wonders
what her father would do.

Before he'd left they'd make these leaps together,
instead she's here reimagining
his small hands, his finger-bones.

The Rain That Began Elsewhere

I traced a stitch raised by your absence.
    I concentrated on this panel of sky
and wound myself into a ribbon of silence.

I have sat at the brink drafting a lie.
    I have held my breath, entered the rooms,
drawn down the blinds and opened my eyes.

I've stood still enough to find my own way home.
    I died a little when I took tiny sips of Spring
and spared no thought for when it all had gone.

I know all I need to know. I breathe in
    the shadow's scent when it is near
and commit it to my own silent skin.

I rest on the tilted fence to prepare
for rain, the rain that began elsewhere.

Gloves

After the *gelato* we walked to the Leather Quarter and into a shop which specialised in gloves. It was an absolutely tiny shop and it had these glass counters where you were supposed to place your elbow and raise your hands in the air. The uniformed assistants knew your glove size with just one glance, of course, and the customers would point at items they wanted to try and they would quickly unwrap one and place it expertly on your hands. She and I had tried on so many gloves and were laughing because it was baking inside this shop and I had a pile of rabbit-lined gloves by my side and she had chosen soft butter lambskin. The shop reeked of tannin and leather. When we returned to our little guesthouse the woman who managed it asked us about our day in very good English. She passed us a leaflet on Siena and it was then that we noticed that her left hand was missing. In fact a good portion of her arm was missing below her elbow and the skin had been neatly tucked and folded under. She didn't seem at all disadvantaged and managed to type on her keyboard and do her job perfectly well. When we got to our room, I started to get ready for dinner. The gloves were laid out on the sideboard. 'Did you see that woman's arm?' she said. 'I want you to get rid of the gloves. I don't want to look at them or even to share the room with them.' She walked to the balcony, and took up a position on a chair and wrapped herself with her shawl. I realised it was pointless trying to argue with her. It's beginning to rain. Somewhere there is a soft hum of an engine on a road far from us. I pick up the gloves and head down to the car and when I look up, she's still sitting there in the fine rain, wrapped up in that stupid shawl and she's crying, not caring if the wind disturbs her face.

My Father Wants to be a Rooftop Railway Surfer

A fly's crushed body has marked
a point between Hyderabad and Delhi.
He lives there in his dreams.
Under a different light, before partition
he was a boy in the *haveli* courtyard
tracing the looped script of an ancestor
or memorising each chink of his mother's
braid on a night they stooped to
collect fireflies.

He shuffles to bed,
complains about the whistling in his head,
inspects his chapped hands.
'This country with all its wind
and broken buds.'
He's not going back.
He wants to sit amongst the stars,
turn his head and see nothing but an
unknown city glinting far behind him.

Ghazal

I thought you my bird and built
you a nest in my heart.
    – Arab Saying

Breathe me in this disheveled night; I go unnoticed.
The air's turned strange and solid, but only I will notice.

If I allow beams of light to pass through the pinholes of my torso
and if light strikes the wall on the other side, would you notice?

Tonight you're three parts God and one part sandalwood dust.
I keep catching your scent by the window, I always notice.

My words pile up like prophets on the point of my tongue.
What passes for transparency are those things you don't notice.

I steal robin's eggs and sketch powder-down feathers for you;
my pocket heats a pulsing nest; the creatures never even notice.

If you could let me bangle my arms around you, rain would fall.
It would speck my lips, my open fingers: then you'd notice.

Instead my eye remains locked in the platinum part of the flower;
the highest branches are the only living things to notice.

Ghazal

Not even our eyes are our own ...
– Frederico García Lorca,
The House of Bernarda Alba

I want to tune in to the surface, beside the mayfly
listen to how she holds her decorum on the skin of the pond.

I want to sequester words, hold them in stress positions,
foreignate them, string them up to ripen on vines

and I want to commune with rain and for the rain
to be merciful, a million tiny pressures on my flesh.

I refuse to return as either rose or tulip but wish
to be planted under the desiring night sky.

I want to be concentrated to a line under the pleat of your palm
and for it to radiate opalesque under shadow.

I want God's fingers to break and for you to watch
as I fold my sleeve, reveal each detail of my paling wrist.

Ode to a Pomegranate

Sweet sequins
turned strange and delicate,
such feverish capsules!

Sita's shy dowry stones.
And rubies, brilliant rubies,
vials of pure narcotic, secreted
by fragments of daybreak.

Fat drops of rain
captured
in your tiny pink purses.

You are such found things:
many estranged souls,
unborns ticking
in blisters of heat.
Our own misremembered
firelit tongues or
chambers of
caught songs.

And an infant globe,
in our palms, shows us
the vastness of things,
turmoil of the earth –
who knows what memory
is stored in its skin
like the tips
of my mother's fingernails

opening, cleaving, intimate with you.

Bulbul

Bulbul, don't look so nervous.
I know the light can be brutal
but let me apply

angled lines of *sindoor* on your
throat, along your breast and
dot your lifted brow.

I imagine capturing you under my
anglepoise, *Bulbul,* coaxing
your wings to flare

and settle on my palm,
deepening the colour
of my hands.

I watch you
through the gap
in the window screen:

your compacted heart receives
the broken bread
whilst the rain nibbles

at the blossom,
you gaze at a bud,
listening hard for a miracle.

Parvati Waits for the Return of Shiva, After the Slaying of Ganesh.

Parvati created Ganesh during Shiva's long absence when she grew lonely. He grew into an obedient, caring child. When Shiva returned one day he did not know or recognise Ganesh and cut off his head. When he realised his terrible mistake he was stricken with remorse and decreed that the head of the first living creature he found would be fused to the body of his son. The first creature that they came across was a baby elephant.

'Beautiful son, your feet are still warm.
Your fleshy thumb is moist from your
little mouth. Child, who I grew not in my
belly but on my belly; each finger was rolled
and pressed in my lap, your limbs oiled
from the sweat of my lip, and the shine on
my collarbone became the mortar to bind you.
The day I announced you the sky offered
me all the birds to devour. You may stop
rehearsing stillness. You and I are the only
gleaming objects in this indecipherable
blackness, beside the plum tree. Do not
be afraid to know yourself, hold melody
in your pores, let me kiss you where your mouth
will be and leave a gold clot on your lip.

Sisters! I will refuse to see ashes today.
Why remove my gold? Who marked my wrists
with violet bangles? You must tell the ghosts.
They are leaving their stinking cages and I'm on
my knees praying they'll not come any closer.
Ghosts with measuring cups who are streaming
through the flowers, can't you see that
this season's plum tree has borne so many
and that beside it lies my son, my headless son
who glints and sings, whose blood still sings?'

Lost Poem

*Geologists from the University of Sydney discovered that
Sandy Island a 26km-wide island in the Pacific Ocean that
can be seen on charts and maps, does not in fact exist.*

The Guardian

Into the soft I go.
Under your cheek
slide in and find
the erratum slip
of a tongue.

*

Migrant in the mouth.
And the smell of yellow
decaying leaves,
spiced milk in steel cups,
my mother's yard of hair.

*

Your eye a drill –
your iris so close to
the surface skims
a sea rippling with
negatives.

*

Language in a tilted room
that gently seeps. And I compare
babies to the size of mothballs
… walnuts.

*

I'm taking in the waters
in the old tradition.
I'm taking in language
through my skin.

Large and Imprecise Baby

I gave birth to a large and imprecise baby
which I'll admit was quite a shock given
my fine distinct bones and on account
of the fact that I didn't even go to term.
One of the mothers in the playgroup gasped
when she saw me unbuckling the buggy
and heaving him into the sandpit.
He never cries or emits any sound
except when immersed in water.
Sometimes I take him to the coast
where he lies passively feeding
from the bottom of the ocean.
I asked that he be referred to a consultant.
The baby watched and pushed raisins
into his mouth whilst Dr Frankel measured
my head with a cold metal instrument.
'It's not him it's you,' he says, eyeing me
suspiciously, stroking his beard.
Outside, I smooth myself down,
kneel to his level and decide to kiss my boy.
As my face nears his, his feeble mouth
makes a jittery noise like a broken gull,
or the scrape of a heavy chair
just as the thin rain starts to fall.

Wireman

On Reduit Beach, St Lucia

Wireman wants to know whether he can fashion me a wire doggy, wire flower or wire soap-dish? I stand with my half-eaten bagel and flip-flops in Wireman's long shadow. I return to my wire house where I live with my wire husband and our wire daughters who wear wire wreaths in their hair and we live on the edge of a sea where there are real wire cuttlefish which gyrate at the bottom of the water. In my belly a new wire thing is simmering, caged in heat whilst blackbirds ooze and oil the sky, the air is spiked with iron filings and the wind will not lift. My daughters raise up their pretty wire necks to the vibrating coiled disc they call the sun. And I look towards the set of mountains where they will make marriages with wiremen. And the moon is soft and just an idea and we all spend our afternoons in the polluted shade of the rusting wire tree, not working on our sea equations or chasing the scent of bougainvillea but attending to our rituals of looking for those hard wire grubs in the wiry undergrowth.

Barbule

An opening or an opening of an opening. A junction between two nerve cells. The most distant thing you can see with the naked eye. A spasm or a gap, the residue on a stylus that makes a record jump. The term used for the hardening of infant gums during teething. The first blind rooting tips of a shoot. The effect of moonlight on an oblong pond and an early word for virgin wool. An out of fashion raised cross-stitch (often associated with shrouds). A neglected silk worm that dies in its cocoon. The foul breath of an exotic bird, most commonly the peacock. Things you may find in winter boots, clouds of tissue, a set of long laces tied with a reef knot, perishing bands of elastic.

The Found Thing

It infiltrated, left a trace in my mouth
and I wanted it. Emboldened, it began
to colonise all those tight spaces.
So I let it bed itself under my fingernails
and drip into my tear-ducts. It felt so warm,
was my constant mute companion,
became one of us, on sports days,
shopping trips, vacations. I never asked
any questions, never wished to see its face.
One morning it was just not there.
I searched and searched, panic rising up
in my throat, and I couldn't manage
to say what it was I had lost, and how.

Woman at Window

It's Decemberish and raining.
The kiss you left on my eyelashes
is dying down.

Everything has changed.
The window shows me clouds
that have not altered,

the sky is jaundiced yet refuses
to stain the light.
Meanwhile your morning progresses

and under some other light you're
tapping out data,
or smoking outside a doorway.

Down below a man continues sweeping,
collecting fallen things. I contemplate window glass,
quietly fracturing on its own terms.

Mr Beeharry's Marriage Bureau

Seated opposite me there is a small woman in a green sari. Her son is about five and she is hand feeding him morsels from a clear tupperware box. The receptionist brings me tea and a clipboard with the forms attached and she lends me her pen which is silver and heavy. I flick through waiting room magazines. My name is called and as I stand up, the small woman stops and stares at me. I remember thinking how very lovely her lashes are. I had already been told that I should be very respectful and call him Doctor. I shake the hand of the white-haired man and give a little half-bow and he acknowledges my show of politeness by nodding slowly then points to the chair. I sit down. He has kind eyes. The examination is brief; he asks me if I have any questions or concerns and I reply no – that everything has been explained to me just fine (and I don't want to be any trouble) and then he takes a piece of square paper from the pile on his desk, scribbles something down, opens a small cubbyhole which is set in the wall and places the note inside it. Then he gestures to a sort of dressing area where there is a blue folding screen and says that I should change now as it will be easier for me later to get to the other side. When I reappear, I notice the room has been rearranged and there are two rows of chairs and sitting on the chairs are my parents, close family and friends. They are smiling at me encouragingly. I turn to them and give them a little wave. The doctor asks if I am ready now, and I say yes and lie down in my white nightie and offer him my arm.

Mrs M Unravels

These cookies are in-store baked for 'extra freshness'.

'I don't want to teach you to suck eggs,'
    I say 'but from where I stand (and I am
standing pouring out the tea) 'Mrs. M,

we share the same enigmatic bone don't we?'
    and in my altered state of alteredness
I believe it sincerely. 'I beg to differ …'

she raises a finger, and then drifts off to search
    for that alluring word (and returns without it).
'As it happens, I have never lost anything

the same way twice, but the thing about a cave
    is its caveness.' This sounds to me like a morally
sound proposition and I nod sagely.

'I remember,' she says (not to me but more
    to herself) 'we never did finish that game of solitaire.
I just don't know why we don't bake any more.'

She places her hands on the table. They resemble
    upturned autumn leaves. 'I was sure of his hands
once, the pressure of his hands.' She's looking

at her old pair of hands, a bit of her shadow dribbles
out of her. I finger the cellophane. 'I'll open them shall I?'

Hummingbird

Ask the stems in the glass to bend.
Let your fingers fly, a momentary grasp

slip into spaces, surge in and out of folds
where breasts begin to curve and rise.

Be God. Press your curing skin to mine,
dissolve and pronounce me. Let my eyes

fall out and embed in the carpet, rooting;
my hands arrange the air for you, braiding.

Reluctant sun at the window, open your eyes
burn through the haze with your severe love.

Slide open the bone-zip of my spine,
anoint each rigid peak. Take my limbs

and fold me over. Here's my mouth, hummingbird,
linger there, and hold my breath.

Ballad of the Small-boned Daughter

I've woken in this fearful flood
    I've woken in the water
Oh mother did you put me here,
    your first-born only daughter?

And can it be that the fishes here
    are nibbling at my flesh?
And can it be the sun I see
    that faces me in death?

'You are as beautiful my *Jaan*
    as the words or tears I'll shed'
as she warmed the blade against
    her cheek, fine as silken thread.

She disarmed her tongue with one
    fine stroke, father held her down.
Then a gloved fist, sealed her in
    and dropped her in to drown.

At first the light protested,
    strained to touch her face,
yet she died again in the waters
    like a disappearing voice.

For six long months she lay like this
    whilst the air pulsed with life.
Then in February they found her
    under a rippling rod of ice.

The mourners came to pay respects
    the mother wailed in white.
The mother had rehearsed sadness
    in the mirror all through the night.

Sometimes her daughter came to her
    in snow or quiet weather.
She avoided the ghost who smelt
    like her small-boned baby daughter.

She couldn't ignore flakes of skin
    and hair filling up her bed.
Nightly she lifted the black strands,
    then went to sleep and bled.

Unwieldy daughter let me be!
    She cried with her voice of wire
You despised all filial duty –
    it's the devil you admire!

One day when the grieving mother
    was blowing on her tea,
they came for her and the father
    and asked them how they'd plead.

We know not how she met her fate,
    how she claimed her watery bed.
The only crime we're guilty of
    was not to see her wed.

Screens showed the trial in detail,
    we followed every note.
We learned about her bloody death,
    how they practised knots in rope.

And yes the parents were found guilty
    for this was a tale of sin
but who grieves for this girl of seventeen
    if not her kith and kin?

Sometimes on a September path
    when you're near or hear the water,
press your minds to the open sky,
    think of the small-boned daughter.

Acknowledgments

Many thanks to the editors of the following publications where some of these poems appeared, sometimes in previous versions: *Poetry Review, The Rialto, Magma, Under the Radar, Toe-Good Poetry, The Lighthouse Magazine* and *The Morning Post. Woman at Window* was published in 2013 in the Templar Anthology *Pelaton.* The poems *Notes Towards an Elegy, My Brother's Body, The Bird* and *Phone Call on a Train Journey* appeared in *Ten: The New Wave* (Bloodaxe 2014), edited by Karen McCarthy Woolf. *Hummingbird* won first prize in the inaugural Magma poetry competition in 2011. *Bad Day in the Office* won second prize in the Troubadour International Poetry Prize in 2013. A portfolio of five of these poems was joint winner of the 2014 Manchester Poetry Prize.

I am very grateful to the following people who sustained me through the writing of the manuscript; Maryam Najand, Vijay Kapoor, Meera Betab, Viney Jung and Sathnam Sanghera. Thank you also to all my tutors at the UEA, as well as my fellow students particularly Stuart Charlesworth who kindly commented on early drafts. Deepest thanks also to my fellow poets at the Poetry School (Versification and APW courses). I wish to note my gratitude to everyone on the *Complete Works Program* and the Arts Council for funding it. Particular thanks to the guidance and encouragement of Nathalie Teitler, Malika Booker and Daljit Nagra.

I am deeply indebted to Mimi Khalvati for her insightfulness and her generosity. Heart-felt thanks to Deryn Rees-Jones and Chloe Johnson, and to all at LUP. Lastly, I am deeply grateful to my family, especially my daughters and my parents for their unending patience and to Stephen for his understanding whilst I was writing these poems.

A note about the Author

Mona Arshi was born to Punjabi Sikh parents in West London where she still lives. She initially trained as a lawyer and worked for Liberty, the UK human rights organisation for several years, undertaking test case litigation under the Human Rights Act. She began writing poetry in 2008 and received a Masters in Creative Writing from the University of East Anglia. She won the inaugural Magma Poetry competition in 2011 and was on the Complete Works Program, a scheme funded by the Arts Council. Mona was also joint winner of the Manchester Creative writing poetry prize in 2014.